SPECIAL ★OPS II★

CIA Paramilitary Operatives in Action

by Jessica Rudolph

Consultant: Fred Pushies
U.S. Special Operations Forces Adviser

BEARPORT
PUBLISHING

New York, New York

Credits

Cover and Title Page, © Pool/Getty Images; 4TR, Courtesy of the Greer Foundation; 4–5, © Zastolskiy Victor/Shutterstock; 5, © Allauddin Khan/Associated Press; 6, © AFP/ Getty Images; 7, © EPA/Sergei Ilnitsky; 8, © Northfoto/Shutterstock; 9, © AP Photo/US Military, Capt. Tommy Avilucea; 10, © Glow Images/Alamy; 11, © Best Images/Fotolia. com; 12, © Shepherd Johnson; 13, © Vasiliy Koval; 14, © Associated Press; 15, © Three Lions/Stringer; 16, © Dan Howell/Shutterstock; 17, © USAF; 18, © AFP/Newscom; 19, © Zohra Bensemra/REUTERS; 20, 21, © AFP/Getty Images; 22, © Anja Niedringhaus; 23, © Associated Press; 24, Courtesy of Johnny Spann; 25, © apelletr/iStockphoto; 26, 27, © Alex Wong/Getty Images; 28T, © Martin Spurny/Shutterstock; 28B, 29TL, © iStockphoto/ Thinkstock; 29TR, © Rama/WIKIMEDIA; 29B, © Rockwell Collins.

Publisher: Kenn Goin
Senior Editor: Joyce Tavolacci
Creative Director: Spencer Brinker
Design: Debrah Kaiser
Photo Researcher: We Research Pictures, LLC

Library of Congress Cataloging-in-Publication Data

Rudolph, Jessica.
    CIA paramilitary operatives in action / by Jessica Rudolph.
        p cm. — (Special ops II)
    Includes bibliographical references and index.
    Audience: Ages 7–12.
    ISBN-13: 978-1-61772-892-1 (library binding) — ISBN-10: 1-61772-892-6 (library binding)
    1. Special forces—United States—Juvenile literature. 2. Paramilitary forces—United States— Juvenile literature. 3. United States. Central Intelligence Agency—Juvenile literature. 4. Terrorism—Prevention—Juvenile literature. I. Title.
    UA34.S64R84 2014
    327.1273—dc23
                                2013007942

For more information, write to Bearport Publishing Company, Inc., 45 West 21st Street, Suite 3B, New York, New York 10010. Printed in the United States of America.

10 9 8 7 6 5 4 3 2 1

Contents

Tracking Terrorists

On October 25, 2003, William "Chief" Carlson was on a dangerous **mission** in eastern Afghanistan. He and other CIA **paramilitary operatives**, or ops, were tracking down **terrorists** in the mountains. Chief and his team sped down a steep, rugged road in their **Humvee**. He had no idea the enemy was lurking close by . . . waiting to attack.

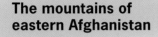

The mountains of eastern Afghanistan

William Carlson was called Chief in honor of his Native American background.

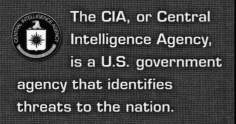

The CIA, or Central Intelligence Agency, is a U.S. government agency that identifies threats to the nation.

Without warning, a **rocket-propelled grenade** (RPG) whizzed through the air. It exploded just inches from the vehicle. Rocks and hot pieces of metal flew everywhere. Chief veered the Humvee into a ditch so his teammates could jump out and take cover. Chief, however, was struck down and killed by gunfire before he could escape.

Enemy fighters in Afghanistan holding an RPG

Helping a Teammate

News of the attack spread to a nearby American military base. A CIA paramilitary op named Christopher Mueller and a group of Afghan **allies** raced to the mountainside. At the battle site, Christopher learned of Chief's death. The two had been good friends. Although he was very upset, Christopher knew there was no time to feel sad. He had to take on the terrorist threat.

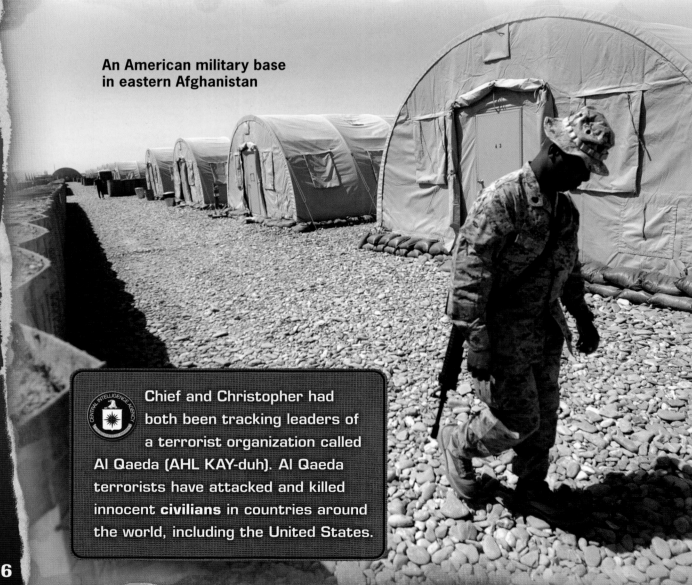

An American military base in eastern Afghanistan

Chief and Christopher had both been tracking leaders of a terrorist organization called Al Qaeda (AHL KAY-duh). Al Qaeda terrorists have attacked and killed innocent **civilians** in countries around the world, including the United States.

As bullets flew around him, Christopher dove for cover. Then he spotted a wounded Afghan ally. Christopher rushed to help his teammate. As he did, a terrorist gunman shot him. The CIA paramilitary op tumbled backward. He tried to get up and keep fighting, but his wounds were too severe. Just like his friend Chief, Christopher died heroically trying to save others.

Chief and Christopher fought alongside Afghan allies, such as these men.

Combat and Intel

CIA paramilitary operatives like Chief and Christopher carry out extremely dangerous missions every day. One of their jobs is to travel to other countries to attack enemy forces. They also destroy enemy supplies, such as weapons. Sometimes, they are even called on to rescue **hostages**.

Special ops during a 2009 hostage rescue in Baghdad, Iraq

CIA paramilitary operatives are not part of the U.S. military. However, they often fight alongside members of the military, especially **special operations forces** such as Navy SEALs.

In addition to **combat** missions, CIA ops have another important job. They gather **intelligence**, or intel. Intel may be a computer file that reveals enemy plans. It could also be a map showing the location of a terrorist training camp. By collecting accurate intel, CIA ops can often help stop the enemy from carrying out a deadly attack.

To help them in their missions, paramilitary ops often train allies, such as these Afghan fighters, and supply them with weapons for battle.

Working in the Shadows

Whatever their mission, operatives must never reveal who they are or what they are doing. Why? If the ops' identities are revealed, their lives might be at risk. **Secrecy** is also needed to complete some missions. If enemies find out about a **covert** plan, they could prevent the ops from carrying it out successfully.

Missions are often planned at CIA headquarters in Langley, Virginia.

To handle covert missions, CIA paramilitary ops have to be tough and smart. They must be able to deal with life-or-death situations without getting nervous. They also need to know how to build relationships with people from different cultures. These skills help them gather valuable intel and train foreign forces.

Operatives don't usually wear uniforms or carry identification that shows their true identity.

CIA paramilitary ops must work well in a group or by themselves. Most missions are carried out by a team of six or fewer paramilitary ops.

Training the Best

The CIA finds only the best people for paramilitary op training. Most **recruits** are soldiers from special operations units, such as Marine Force Recon. These soldiers are experienced fighters. In addition, they are physically and mentally strong.

Paramilitary operative training takes place at secret locations in the United States. One location is believed to be Camp Peary (above), in Virginia.

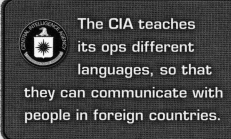

The CIA teaches its ops different languages, so that they can communicate with people in foreign countries.

Training takes about one year. Operatives learn how to deal with almost any situation. For example, they are taught how to break into buildings to collect intel. Ops also learn how to fight hand-to-hand in case they ever lose their weapons. In addition, they take acting lessons. Why? Sometimes, the ops need to convince the enemy to trust them. Therefore, they must be good at making up stories.

Like these soldiers, CIA paramilitary ops are taught hand-to-hand combat.

The Cold War

Paramilitary operatives have been protecting Americans since the CIA was formed in 1947. At that time, the greatest threats to the United States came from countries that wanted to expand **communism** throughout the world. For decades, paramilitary ops helped allies in places like Vietnam and Cuba fight against communist governments.

Fidel Castro was the leader of Cuba from 1959 to 2008.

Cuba is an island nation 90 miles (145 km) off the coast of Florida.

One of the most famous CIA operations took place in 1961. The CIA organized a mission to arm, train, and lead Cuban **rebels**, who wanted to overthrow Cuba's communist government. In April 1961, a small team of CIA paramilitary ops along with about 1,400 rebels attacked Cuba. However, the Cuban government had a much larger military force. In just three days, the invasion was crushed.

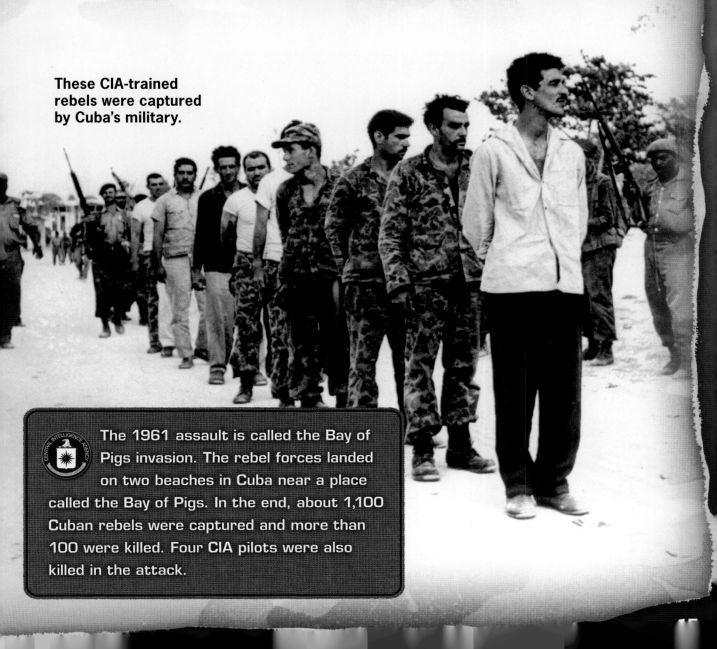

These CIA-trained rebels were captured by Cuba's military.

The 1961 assault is called the Bay of Pigs invasion. The rebel forces landed on two beaches in Cuba near a place called the Bay of Pigs. In the end, about 1,100 Cuban rebels were captured and more than 100 were killed. Four CIA pilots were also killed in the attack.

A New Kind of War

Today, the CIA is fighting a new war—one against terrorists. On September 11, 2001, terrorists attacked the United States, killing thousands of Americans. Al Qaeda, a group based in Afghanistan, organized the attack. It would not be easy for U.S. forces to find Al Qaeda leaders, however. Afghanistan's rulers, the **Taliban**, were protecting them.

The Twin Towers after they were attacked by terrorists on 9/11

The leader of Al Qaeda was Osama bin Laden. He planned the attacks of September 11, 2001. On that day, terrorists **hijacked** four airplanes. Two planes were flown into the Twin Towers in New York City. Another plane smashed into the Pentagon in Virginia. The fourth plane crashed in a Pennsylvania field.

To track down the terrorists, CIA paramilitary operatives secretly slipped into Afghanistan. The operatives worked closely with local allies called the Northern Alliance. As a result, the CIA gathered important intel on the location of Al Qaeda training camps. Paramilitary ops also fought the Taliban army. By December 2001, the Taliban was driven from power.

To get around the steep mountains of Afghanistan, U.S. and Northern Alliance forces often traveled by horse.

Into Iraq

In March 2003, the **War on Terror** expanded to Iraq. Some U.S. officials believed Saddam Hussein, the country's **dictator**, was building powerful weapons to use against Americans. When the U.S. military invaded Iraq, Hussein went into hiding.

Saddam Hussein (center)

In December 2003, CIA paramilitary ops and U.S. military forces located Hussein. He was discovered on a farm near Tikrit, Iraq, hiding in a tiny underground hole. When the U.S. team lifted the trapdoor of his hiding place, Hussein raised his arms to surrender. He said, "I am Saddam Hussein, president of Iraq." The once-powerful dictator was captured!

After his capture, Hussein was put on trial for killing more than 100,000 of his own people. He was found guilty and hanged for his crimes in 2006.

The hole where Saddam Hussein was found hiding

The World's Most Wanted Terrorist

While Saddam Hussein was being captured, U.S. officials were still trying to track down Osama bin Laden. In the years after 9/11, CIA ops collected intel about where Osama bin Laden might be hiding. Eventually, they traced him to a huge **compound** in northern Pakistan. The CIA then carefully planned a covert mission to capture him.

Osama bin Laden

Abbottabad, Pakistan, where bin Laden was hiding

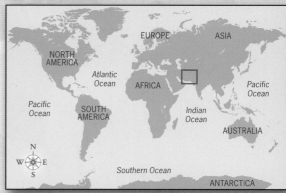

On May 2, 2011, a team of Navy SEALs and CIA paramilitary ops flew to the compound under the cover of night. Once on the ground, they blasted their way inside with explosives. A gun battle broke out. Four terrorists were killed, including their target—bin Laden. The team gathered files, computers, bin Laden's body, and then took off. They carried out the entire mission in less than one hour.

Bin Laden's compound in Pakistan

To avoid being tracked down, bin Laden used a messenger, instead of computers or phones, to communicate with other terrorists. However, CIA ops found the messenger and followed him to the compound.

Prisoner Revolt

Many brave CIA paramilitary operatives have fought in the War on Terror. One of the bravest is Johnny Micheal Spann. On November 25, 2001, Johnny and fellow CIA ops were helping Northern Alliance soldiers in northern Afghanistan. Together, they were guarding almost 500 dangerous Taliban fighters in a mud-walled fort.

The mud-walled fort, built in the 1800s, was used to house several hundred prisoners.

Johnny began **interrogating** some of the prisoners he was guarding. He had hoped to find a Taliban fighter who knew the whereabouts of high-ranking terrorists. Johnny was unaware, however, that a couple of the prisoners were armed.

John Walker Lindh

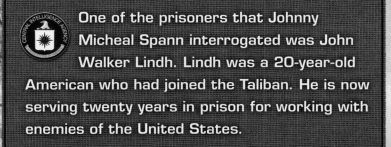

One of the prisoners that Johnny Micheal Spann interrogated was John Walker Lindh. Lindh was a 20-year-old American who had joined the Taliban. He is now serving twenty years in prison for working with enemies of the United States.

Holding His Ground

The two prisoners were hiding grenades, which they threw at Johnny and the other guards. Explosions rocked the fort walls. This attack caused a prison **uprising**. In the chaos, hundreds of prisoners attacked the guards and grabbed their guns.

Johnny Micheal Spann

Johnny could have fled from the charging prisoners, but he held his ground. He aimed his rifle and began shooting. A flood of prisoners barreled toward him. When Johnny ran out of bullets, he fired his pistol. When the pistol bullets were gone, he fought with his bare fists. The enemy force was too great, though. Eventually, Johnny was killed. His brave actions, however, allowed other guards to escape.

Johnny Micheal Spann is buried at Arlington National Cemetery in Virginia.

In just minutes, the prisoners killed several guards and grabbed the rifles, grenades, RPGs, and rockets stored in the fort. It took a week of fighting for American and Northern Alliance forces to take back the fort.

"A Better, Safer World"

Today, Johnny Micheal Spann is honored at CIA headquarters. In the lobby, there is a **memorial** with more than 100 stars carved into it. Each star represents a CIA operative or employee who died protecting others.

IN HONOR OF THOSE MEMBERS
OF THE CENTRAL INTELLIGENCE AGENCY
WHO GAVE THEIR LIVES IN THE SERVICE OF THEIR COUNTRY

In addition to Johnny Micheal Spann, William "Chief" Carlson and Christopher Mueller have stars in their honor on the CIA Memorial Wall.

After Johnny's death, former CIA director George Tenet said, "Johnny understood that it is not enough simply to dream of a better, safer world. He understood that it has to be built—with passion and dedication, in the face of obstacles." This is what all CIA paramilitary ops understand as they stare down danger to save lives.

1998 ★
★

2001 ★ Johnny Micheal Spann

2003 ★ Helge P. Boes
★ Gregg David Wenzel
★ William Francis Carlson
★ Christopher Glenn Mueller

2005 ★

2006 ★ Rachel A. Dean

2008 ★
★

Book of Honor

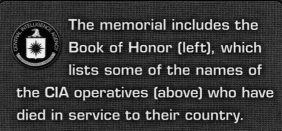

The memorial includes the Book of Honor (left), which lists some of the names of the CIA operatives (above) who have died in service to their country.

CIA Paramilitary Operatives' Gear

CIA paramilitary operatives use lots of equipment to carry out their missions. Here is some of the gear they use.

The CIA uses aircraft such as **MI-17 helicopters** to transport operatives to battle sites.

Operatives sometimes travel in armored vehicles called **Humvees** when carrying out their missions.

The **AK-47 rifle** is one type of gun a paramilitary operative may carry for combat.

Operatives often carry a **pistol** in addition to their rifle.

When CIA paramilitary ops find an enemy base or training camp, they map the location using **GPS equipment**. That information may then be used by the U.S. military to launch attacks against the enemy.

Glossary

allies (AL-eyez) people, groups, or nations that work together for a common cause

civilians (si-VIL-yuhnz) people who are not in the armed forces

combat (KAHM-bat) fighting between people or armies

communism (KOM-yoo-niz-uhm) a system of government in which all goods and property are controlled by one group

compound (KOM-pound) a walled-in area with buildings inside

covert (koh-VURT) secret; disguised

dictator (DIK-tay-tur) a person who has complete control over a country and usually runs it unfairly

hijacked (HYE-jakt) took control of illegally

hostages (HOSS-tij-iz) people held prisoner as a way of demanding money or other things

Humvee (hum-VEE) a jeep-like military vehicle that can move troops and travel over rough roads

intelligence (in-TEL-uh-juhnts) information about an enemy

interrogating (in-TER-uh-*gayt*-ing) pressuring a person to gain information

memorial (muh-MOR-ee-uhl) something that is built to remember a person or event

mission (MISH-uhn) an important task

paramilitary operatives (*par*-uh-MIL-uh-ter-ee OP-ruh-tivz) people who have been specially trained to take part in combat missions and gather intelligence

rebels (REB-uhlz) soldiers who are fighting against a government

recruits (ri-KROOTS) people who have recently joined a group

rocket-propelled grenade (ROK-it-pru-PELD gruh-NAYD) a small bomb fired by a rocket often used by insurgents to damage or destroy buildings or vehicles

secrecy (SEE-kra-see) the act of keeping something secret

special operations forces (SPESH-uhl *op*-uh-RAY-shuhnz FORSS-iz) groups of highly skilled soldiers in the military; called special ops for short

Taliban (TAL-ah-ban) a military and political group that ruled Afghanistan from 1996 to 2001

terrorists (TER-ur-ists) individuals or groups that use violence and terror to get what they want

uprising (UHP-*rye*-zing) a revolt or riot

War on Terror (WOR AHN TER-ur) the ongoing military campaign waged by the United States and some of its allies to fight terrorists around the world

Bibliography

Kessler, Ronald. *The CIA at War: Inside the Secret Campaign Against Terror.* New York: St. Martin's Press (2003).

North, Oliver. *American Heroes in Special Operations.* Nashville, TN: Fidelis Books (2010).

Prados, John. *Safe for Democracy: The Secret Wars of the CIA.* Chicago: Ivan R. Dee (2006).

The official Web site of the CIA: www.cia.gov/index.html

Read More

Abraham, Philip. *The CIA (High Interest Books: Top Secret).* New York: Children's Press (2003).

Hamilton, John. *The CIA (Defending the Nation).* Edina, MN: ABDO (2007).

Lunis, Natalie. *The Takedown of Osama bin Laden (Special Ops).* New York: Bearport (2012).

Learn More Online

To learn more about CIA Paramilitary Operatives, visit
www.bearportpublishing.com/SpecialOpsII

Index

About the Author

Jessica Rudolph lives in California. She has edited and written
many children's books about history, literature, science, and nature.